THREE RIVERS PUBLIC LIBRARY DISTRICT
3 1561 00171 9347

D1368318

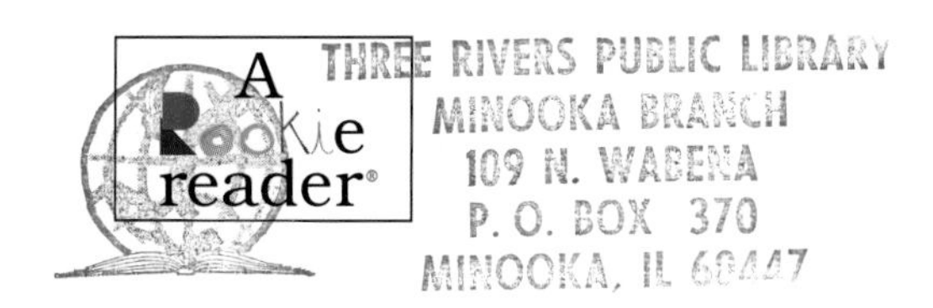

Just Like Always

Written by
Anne M. Perry

Illustrated by
Tammie Lyon

Children's Press®
A Division of Scholastic Inc.
New York • Toronto • London • Auckland • Sydney
Mexico City • New Delhi • Hong Kong
Danbury, Connecticut

For Sarah, whose parents both love her very much.
–A.M.P.

For Linda –thanks for being such a great pal!
–T.L.

Consultant

Eileen Robinson
Reading Specialist

Library of Congress Cataloging-in-Publication Data

Perry, Anne M., 1943-
Just like always / written by Anne M. Perry ; illustrated by Tammie Lyon.
p. cm. – (A rookie reader)
Summary: A girl finds that most things in her life remain the same after her parents' divorce.
ISBN 0-516-25154-6 (lib. bdg.) 0-516-25287-9 (pbk.)

[1. Divorce–Fiction.] I. Lyon, Tammie, ill. II. Title. III. Series.
PZ7.P4348Ju 2005
[E]–dc22

2004013702

Printed in the United States of America.

1 2 3 4 5 6 7 8 9 10 R 14 13 12 11 10 09 08 07 06 05

Mom and Dad love me,
just like always.

Mom lives here.

Dad lives here.

Mom gives me hugs and kisses.

Dad does, too.

I visit Grandma and Grandpa.

I visit Nana, too.

Some things are different. Mom and I live together during the week.

I visit Dad on weekends.

Sometimes I help Mom and Dad work.

We shop and cook.

Mom and I hike.

Dad and I fish.

We like to read.

Mom and I garden.

Dad takes me to a baseball game.

Mom goes to campouts.

Dad coaches soccer.
Mom watches me play.

Mom takes me to dance class.

Dad watches me dance.

They visit my teacher
at school together.

They are proud of me.

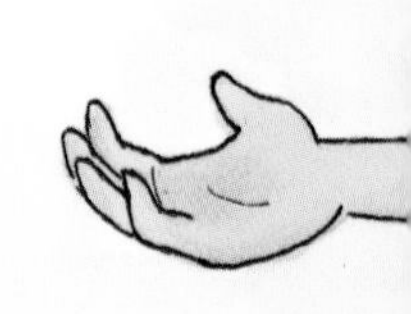

A++

They love me very much.

Just like always.

Word List (63 words)

a	does	I	on	things
always	during	just	play	to
and	fish	kisses	proud	together
are	game	like	read	too
at	garden	live	school	very
baseball	gives	lives	shop	visit
campouts	goes	love	soccer	watches
class	Grandma	me	some	we
coaches	Grandpa	Mom	sometimes	week
cook	help	much	takes	weekends
Dad	here	my	teacher	work
dance	hike	Nana	the	
different	hugs	of	they	

About the Author

Dr. Anne M. Perry lives near College Station, Texas. She has taught children, levels K-8, and at the university level, for 35 years before retiring to write in 2001. She and her husband, Frank, enjoy photography, writing, fishing, attending church, and riding his motorcycle. They have two grown children, four grandchildren, and two step-grandchildren, whom they love very much.

About the Illustrator

Tammie Lyon has illustrated numerous children's books, including a title chosen for the American Booksellers Association Pick of the Lists. She lives in Cincinnati, Ohio, with her husband Lee, and her dogs Moe and Gus.